Usborne

My First Book About

Nature

Usborne Quicklinks

To visit websites with video clips, activities and fun facts
about nature, go to www.usborne.com/quicklinks and type
in the keywords "first book about nature".

Website researcher: Jacqui Clark

Expert advice from Dr. John Rostron and Dr. Margaret Rostron

Contents

My First Book About

Nature

Felicity Brooks and Caroline Young

Illustrated by Mar Ferrero

Edited by Hannah Watson

Designed by
Francesca Allen and
Kirsty Tizzard

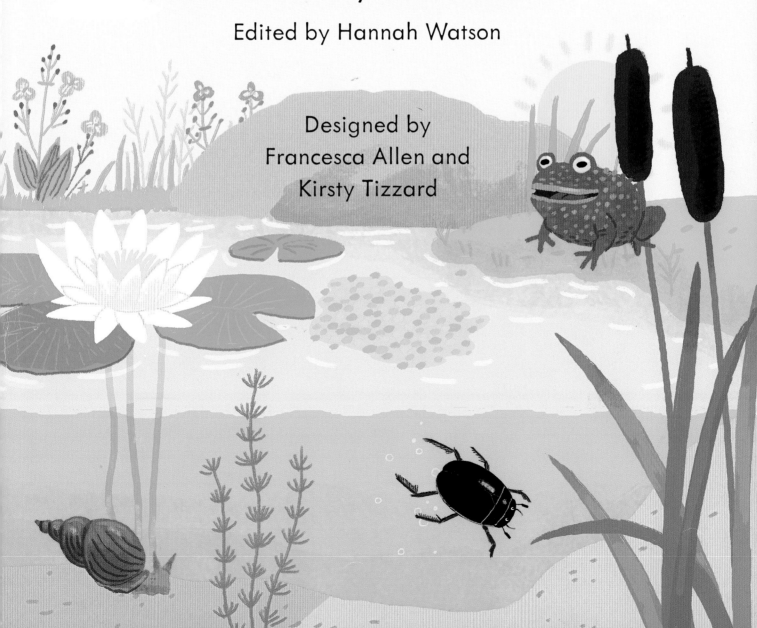

What is nature?

Nature is all the living things on the Earth. Trees, plants, animals, birds, fish and bugs are all part of nature, and so are you.

squirrel

bird

There's lots to see if you go for a walk in the autumn.

fallen leaves

toadstools

web

Look for all the things that live on an old rotting log.

4

Make a nature table

These are the kinds of things you could collect to put on a nature table.

A snail lived in this shell.

This leaf may have been nibbled by insects.

This feather comes from a bird called a wood pigeon.

Moss is a plant that can grow in damp, shady places.

A dormouse made a hole in this nutshell.

These catkins are the flowers of a birch tree.

These are the leaf buds of a tree.

Pine cones come from pine trees and may have pine seeds in them.

The crispy stuff growing on this twig is called lichen.

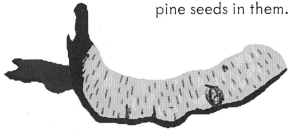

This bark comes from the trunk of a silver birch tree.

A baby bird hatched out of this broken eggshell.

Nature's year

Nature does not stay the same all year.
Can you spot the things that have changed
in these pictures of the four seasons?

Spring

Summer

Do you know the names of these animals?
Answers on page 32.

a)   b)   c)   d)

Autumn

Winter

7

Plants and flowers

People grow plants in parks and gardens, but wild plants grow on their own. All plants need light, water and time to grow.

Here's how a dandelion flower grows from a tiny dandelion seed.

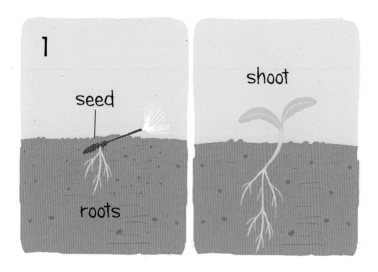

A seed falls on the soil. Roots grow down, the fluffy bit dies and a shoot grows up.

Lots of spiky leaves grow, and then a dandelion flower bud appears.

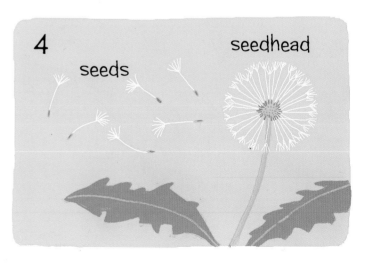

The bud opens into a flower. When the flower dies, a fluffy seedhead is left.

The wind carries the seeds off. They may land on the soil and grow into new plants.

Helpful bees

pollen

The yellow powder in flowers is pollen. Flowers need pollen from another flower to make seeds. Bees help them get some.

If a bee visits a flower looking for food, pollen sticks to its fur. When it visits another flower, some pollen drops off.

These bees are visiting some wildflowers. Which of these flowers do you recognize?

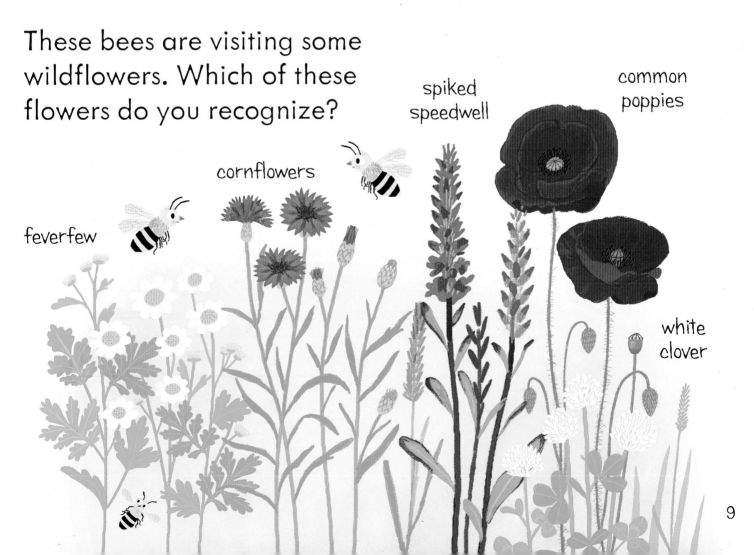

spiked speedwell

common poppies

cornflowers

feverfew

white clover

A bit about trees

Trees are the biggest plants in the world and some are over 1,000 years old. Cover the labels and see if you can name all the parts of this tree.

leaf

trunk

branch

roots

Changing trees

Evergreen trees keep their leaves all year. Others, called deciduous trees, lose their leaves every autumn.

Spring   Summer   Autumn   Winter

Leaves and seeds

Trees grow from seeds and different trees have leaves and seeds of different shapes. Can you match the leaves to their seeds? Answers on page 32.

beech   horse chestnut   oak   maple

maple key   conker   beechnut   acorn

11

Kinds of animals

There are millions of animals in the world, from tiny bugs to huge whales, but they all fit into groups.

bird

Birds have feathers, wings and beaks and lay eggs. Find out more on page 16.

cow

calf

Mammals such as cows give birth to their babies and feed them on their milk.

Bugs and insects are animals too. There's more about them on pages 18 and 19.

insect

Lizards, snakes and other reptiles have dry, scaly skin. Most lay eggs.

snake

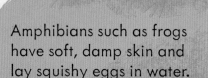

frog

Fish and many other animals live in water. Find out more on pages 22 and 23.

frogspawn

fish

Amphibians such as frogs have soft, damp skin and lay squishy eggs in water.

The six main animal groups

Amphibians

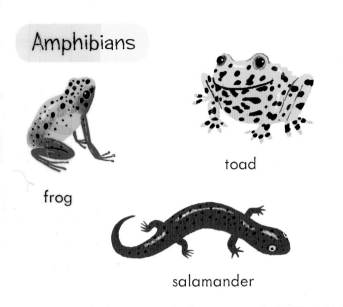

toad

frog

salamander

Birds

toucan

penguin

flamingo

Insects

fly

grasshopper

ant

Mammals

tiger

sheep

whale

Fish

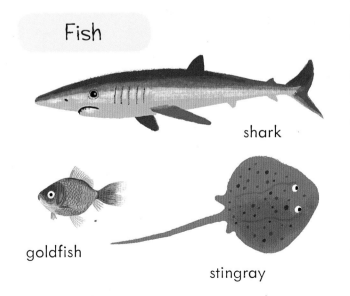

shark

goldfish

stingray

Reptiles

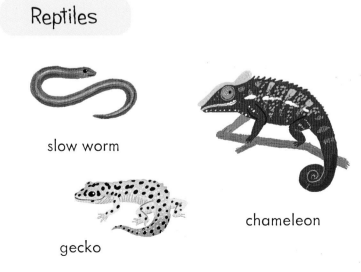

slow worm

chameleon

gecko

More about animals

People feed pet animals, but animals in the wild have to find food or hunt other animals to eat.

Some animals, such as elk, eat only plants. They are known as herbivores.

elk

Carnivores, such as wolves, eat meat or fish. They hunt other animals to eat.

Racoons are omnivores. They eat everything.

wolf

racoon

14

Food chains

A food chain shows who eats what. We are part of some food chains, too.

An arrow from a mole to an owl shows that owls eat moles.

worm

mole

owl

grass

cow

human

What do animals need?

As well as food, animals need air, water, exercise and a safe place to live. Pets must get what they need from people.

Rabbits need clean water to drink.

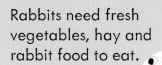
Rabbits need fresh vegetables, hay and rabbit food to eat.

A rabbit needs space to run around and a clean, dry place to rest.

All about birds

Birds live all over the world and come in many shapes and sizes. Peacocks, eagles, flamingos and parrots are all birds.

The world's biggest birds are ostriches. At 2.8m (9.2ft) tall, they are much taller than grown-ups.

This is the actual size of a bee hummingbird, the smallest bird. It's only 5cm (2in) long from beak to tail.

Bird words

Whatever their shape and size, all birds have a beak, wings and feathers, and they all lay eggs.

This bird is called an oriole. Orioles can often be found high up in large, leafy trees in parts of North America.

beak

Birds grow a new set of feathers every year.

wing

breast

claws

tail

feather

Here are some birds that may visit gardens around the world.

pigeon

magpie

If you put some food out for wild birds, they may visit more often.

starling

goldfinch

thrush

sparrow

Baby birds

Many birds build cosy homes called nests from grass, twigs and moss.

A mother bird lays eggs in the nest. When they hatch, tiny chicks come out.

The parent birds bring food to the chicks until they are ready to fly.

Insects and bugs

Wherever you live, tiny animals are all around and many of them are insects. Over a million kinds have been discovered so far.

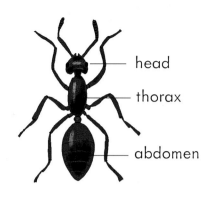

Insects have a head, six legs and a two-part body.

This garden is full of bugs, slugs and other little animals. Which ones do you think are insects? Answers on page 32.

spider

peacock butterfly

wasp

Butterflies visit flowers to drink a sweet liquid called nectar.

slug

worm

ants

From egg to butterfly

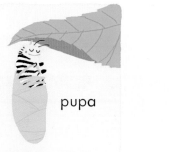

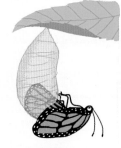

A butterfly lays eggs on a plant. Tiny caterpillars come out of them.

A caterpillar eats and eats and grows fast, then it hangs down from a plant.

A case called a pupa forms from its body and its skin falls off.

After a few weeks, the pupa breaks open. A butterfly comes out.

Which of these little animals do you recognize?

moth

shieldbug

bee

ladybird

woodlouse

snail

caterpillar

earwig

The deep dark sea

The further down you go in the sea, the colder and darker it gets. Different kinds of plants and animals live in each layer or 'zone'.

All sorts of fish, dolphins and whales live in the sunlit zone, along with all the plants.

humpback whale

This is the twilight zone. It only gets a little light, but some kinds of sea animals live here.

swordfish

flashlight fish

hatchet fish

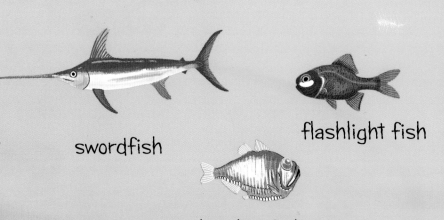

In the sunless zone, it's dark and the water is just above freezing. Only a few kinds of animals live here.

vampire squid

The abyssal zone is icy cold and dark all the time. Some strange fish live down here.

gulper eel

Seabirds dive into the water to catch fish.

tuna

dolphin

jellyfish

basking shark

turtle

This is a coral reef.

squid

sperm whale

sunlit zone

twilight zone

black swallower

cookiecutter shark

sunless zone

tripod fish

abyssal zone

anglerfish

By the water

Ponds, lakes and rivers are home to all kinds of creatures. Here are some to look for around a pond.

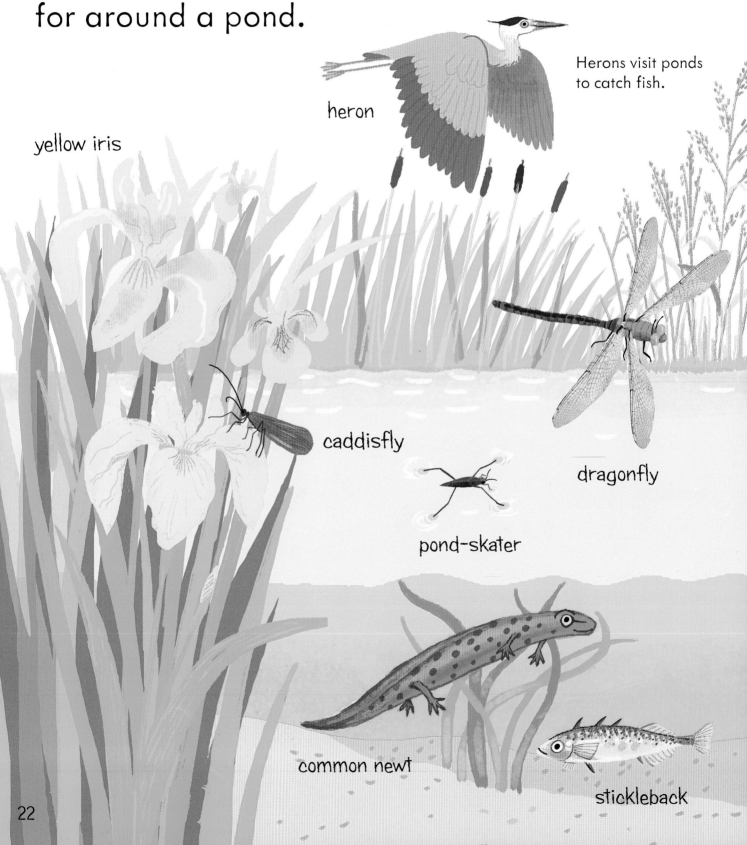

Herons visit ponds to catch fish.

heron

yellow iris

caddisfly

pond-skater

dragonfly

common newt

stickleback

Tadpoles and frogs

tadpole

frog

Frogs lay tiny eggs covered in jelly in water. It's called frogspawn.

Baby frogs called tadpoles grow in the jelly. Then they nibble a way out.

Tadpoles start to grow legs and then their tails get shorter.

Finally their tails disappear. Now the tadpoles have become tiny frogs.

greater reedmace

damselfly

common toad

waterlily

duckweed

great pond snail

great diving beetle

On the beach

When the sea goes out, pools of water are left between the rocks on a beach. Many plants and animals live in these pools. Here are a few you might spot.

seagulls

sea

sand

rock

limpet

periwinkles

seaweed

sea anemone

crab

starfish

blenny

Beach treasures

These are some things you might find on a beach.
Which one shouldn't be here? Find out on page 32.

seashells

Razor-shells are long and thin. What other shell shapes can you see?

People sometimes call these cases 'mermaid's purses'.

egg case of a ray

These cases contained the eggs of fish called rays and dogfish.

plastic bottle top

A cuttlebone is the inside shell of a cuttlefish.

Sand dollars are animals similar to starfish.

sand dollar

cuttlebone

seaweed

driftwood

pebbles

Herring gulls visit the beach looking for food.

25

Animal tracks

Some animals have walked, run, or hopped across this page and left their tracks.

bear

See if you can spot any animal tracks next time you are out for a walk.

horse

fox

rabbit

bird

mouse

Nature quiz

How much have you learned about nature?
Find out by doing this quiz. You can look back through
the book to help you, if you like. Answers on page 32.

1. Which of these animals are mammals?

a) tiger   b) pigeon   c) goldfish   d) whale

2. Which of these belong under the sea?

a) water lily   b) turtle   c) dolphin   d) frog   e) jellyfish

3. This food chain has been muddled up.
   Put it in the correct order to show who eats what.

a) human   b) grass   c) cow

Spotting game

Can you find all of these things in the book?
Which man-made object is the odd one out?

flamingo   maple leaf   gecko   bird feeder   seashell

conker   starfish   damselfly   poppy   pine cone

Changing nature

Can you remember what each of the things
in the top row will become?

1) frogspawn   2) acorn   3) caterpillar   4) egg

a) bird   b) frog   c) oak tree   d) butterfly

Glossary

amphibian – an animal with soft, damp skin which can live on land and in water.

carnivore – an animal which eats meat or fish. Carnivores hunt other animals to eat.

deciduous – a type of tree which loses its leaves every autumn.

egg – an object laid by female animals, such as birds, reptiles and fish, from which a baby animal will hatch.

evergreen – a type of tree which keeps its leaves all year round.

food chain – a way of showing how animals are linked to each other by the plants or animals they eat.

herbivore – an animal which only eats plants.

insect – a small animal with six legs, a two-part body and a head.

mammal – an animal which normally gives birth to live babies and feeds them on its milk.

man-made – to do with things made by people, such as cars and houses.

nature – all things not made by people, including rocks, rivers and mountains as well as living things such as plants and animals.

nectar – a sweet liquid which attracts birds and insects to flowers.

omnivore – an animal which eats plants and animals.

pollen – a powder from plants which they need to make seeds.

reptile – an animal with dry, scaly skin. Most reptiles lay eggs.

root – part of a plant which grows in the soil and holds the plant in place. Roots take water and some food from the soil.

season – one of the four parts the year is divided into: spring, summer, autumn and winter.

seed – part of a plant which can grow into a new plant.

Index

Answers

p.7 Name the animals a) hedgehog; b) bird; c) squirrel; d) fox

p.11 Which tree? beech and beechnut; horse chestnut and conker; oak and acorn; maple and maple key.

p.18 Which are insects? Butterflies, moths, ants, bees, wasps, shieldbugs, earwigs and ladybirds are all insects.

p.25 Beach treasures The plastic bottle top is litter. It shouldn't be on the beach.

p.27 Nature quiz 1. a, d; 2. b, c, e; 3. b, c, a.

p.28 Spotting game flamingo p.13; maple leaf p.11; gecko p.13; bird feeder p.17; seashell p.25; conker p.11; starfish p.24; damselfly p.23; poppy p.9; pine cone p.5. The bird feeder is the odd one out as it is man-made.

p.28 Changing nature 1. b; 2. c; 3. d; 4. a